Thomas Edison

A Biography

Editor

Landen Garland

Scribbles

Year of Publication 2018

ISBN : 9789352979639

Book Published by

Scribbles

(An Imprint of Alpha Editions)

email - alphaedis@gmail.com

Produced by: PediaPress GmbH
Limburg an der Lahn
Germany
http://pediapress.com/

The content within this book was generated collaboratively by volunteers. Please be advised that nothing found here has necessarily been reviewed by people with the expertise required to provide you with complete, accurate or reliable information. Some information in this book may be misleading or simply wrong. Alpha Editions and PediaPress does not guarantee the validity of the information found here. If you need specific advice (for example, medical, legal, financial, or risk management) please seek a professional who is licensed or knowledgeable in that area.

Sources, licenses and contributors of the articles and images are listed in the section entitled "References". Parts of the books may be licensed under the GNU Free Documentation License. A copy of this license is included in the section entitled "GNU Free Documentation License"

The views and characters expressed in the book are those of the contributors and his/her imagination and do not represent the views of the Publisher.

Contents

Articles   **1**

    Thomas Edison 1

Appendix   **37**

    References 37

    Article Sources and Contributors 40

    Image Sources, Licenses and Contributors 41

Article Licenses   **43**

Index   **45**

Thomas Edison

<indicator name="pp-default"> 🔒 </indicator>

Thomas Edison	
 Edison, c.1922	
Born	Thomas Alva Edison February 11, 1847 Milan, Ohio, U.S.
Died	October 18, 1931 (aged 84) West Orange, New Jersey, U.S.
Burial place	Thomas Edison National Historical Park
Nationality	American
Education	Self-educated
Occupation	Inventor, businessman
Years active	1877–1930
Spouse(s)	• Mary Stilwell (m. 1871–1884) • Mina Miller (m. 1886–1931)
Children	• Marion Estelle Edison (1873–1965) • Thomas Alva Edison Jr. (1876–1935) • William Leslie Edison (1878–1937) • Madeleine Edison (1888–1979) • Charles Edison (1890–1969) • Theodore Miller Edison (1898–1992)
Parent(s)	• Samuel Ogden Edison Jr. (1804–1896) • Nancy Matthews Elliott (1810–1871)
Relatives	Lewis Miller (father-in-law)
Signature	

Thomas Alva Edison (February 11, 1847 – October 18, 1931) was an American inventor and businessman, who has been described as America's greatest inventor. He is credited with developing many devices in fields such as electric power generation, mass communication, sound recording, and motion pictures. These inventions, which include the phonograph, the motion picture camera, and the long-lasting, practical electric light bulb, had a widespread impact on the modern industrialized world. He was one of the first inventors to apply the principles of mass production and teamwork to the process of invention, working with many researchers and employees. He is often credited with establishing the first industrial research laboratory.

Edison was raised in the American midwest and early in his career he worked as a telegraph operator, which inspired some of his earliest inventions. In 1876, he established his first laboratory facility in Menlo Park, New Jersey, where many of his early inventions would be developed. He would later establish a botanic laboratory in Fort Myers, Florida in collaboration with businessmen Henry Ford and Harvey Firestone, and a laboratory in West Orange, New Jersey that featured the world's first film studio, the Black Maria. He was a prolific inventor, holding 1,093 US patents in his name, as well as patents in other countries. Edison married twice and fathered six children. He died in 1931 of complications with diabetes.

Early life

Thomas Edison was born, in 1847, in Milan, Ohio, and grew up in Port Huron, Michigan. He was the seventh and last child of Samuel Ogden Edison Jr. (1804–1896, born in Marshalltown, Nova Scotia) and Nancy Matthews Elliott (1810–1871, born in Chenango County, New York).[1] His father, the son of a Loyalist refugee, had moved as a boy with the family from Nova Scotia, settling in southwestern Ontario (then called Upper Canada), in a village known as Shewsbury, later Vienna, by 1811. Samuel Jr. eventually fled Ontario, because he took part in the unsuccessful Mackenzie Rebellion of 1837. His father, Samuel Sr., had earlier fought in the War of 1812 as captain of the First Middlesex Regiment. By contrast, Samuel Jr.'s struggle found him on the losing side, and he crossed into the United States at Sarnia-Port Huron. Once across the border, he found his way to Milan, Ohio. His patrilineal family line was Dutch by way of New Jersey; the surname had originally been "Edeson."

Edison only attended school for a few months and was instead taught by his mother. Much of his education came from reading R.G. Parker's *School of Natural Philosophy* and The Cooper Union for the Advancement of Science and Art.

Figure 1: *Edison as a boy*

Edison developed hearing problems at an early age. The cause of his deafness has been attributed to a bout of scarlet fever during childhood and recurring untreated middle-ear infections. Around the middle of his career, Edison attributed the hearing impairment to being struck on the ears by a train conductor when his chemical laboratory in a boxcar caught fire and he was thrown off the train in Smiths Creek, Michigan, along with his apparatus and chemicals. In his later years, he modified the story to say the injury occurred when the conductor, in helping him onto a moving train, lifted him by the ears.[2,3]

Early career

Edison's family moved to Port Huron, Michigan, after the canal owners successfully kept the railroad out of Milan Ohio in 1854 and business declined.[4] Edison sold candy and newspapers on trains running from Port Huron to Detroit, and sold vegetables. He became a telegraph operator after he saved three-year-old Jimmie MacKenzie from being struck by a runaway train. Jimmie's father, station agent J. U. MacKenzie of Mount Clemens, Michigan, was so grateful that he trained Edison as a telegraph operator. Edison's first telegraphy job away from Port Huron was at Stratford Junction, Ontario, on the Grand Trunk Railway.[5] He was held responsible for a near collision. He also studied qualitative analysis and conducted chemical experiments on the train until he left the job.

Edison obtained the exclusive right to sell newspapers on the road, and, with the aid of four assistants, he set in type and printed the *Grand Trunk Herald*, which he sold with his other papers. This began Edison's long streak of entrepreneurial ventures, as he discovered his talents as a businessman. These talents eventually led him to found 14 companies, including General Electric, still one of the largest publicly traded companies in the world.

In 1866, at the age of 19, Edison moved to Louisville, Kentucky, where, as an employee of Western Union, he worked the Associated Press bureau news wire. Edison requested the night shift, which allowed him plenty of time to spend at his two favorite pastimes—reading and experimenting. Eventually, the latter pre-occupation cost him his job. One night in 1867, he was working with a lead–acid battery when he spilled sulfuric acid onto the floor. It ran between the floorboards and onto his boss's desk below. The next morning Edison was fired.[6]

One of his mentors during those early years was a fellow telegrapher and inventor named Franklin Leonard Pope, who allowed the impoverished youth to live and work in the basement of his Elizabeth, New Jersey, home. Some of Edison's earliest inventions were related to telegraphy, including a stock ticker. His first patent was for the electric vote recorder, U.S. Patent 90,646[7], which was granted on June 1, 1869.[8]

Menlo Park laboratory (1876-1886)

Research and development facility

Edison's major innovation was the establishment of an industrial research lab in 1876. It was built in Menlo Park, a part of Raritan Township (now named Edison Township in his honor) in Middlesex County, New Jersey, with the funds from the sale of Edison's quadruplex telegraph. After his demonstration of the telegraph, Edison was not sure that his original plan to sell it for $4,000 to $5,000 was right, so he asked Western Union to make a bid. He was surprised to hear them offer $10,000 ($216,300 in today's dollars.[9]<templatestyles src="Module:Citation/CS1/styles.css"></templatestyles>), which he gratefully accepted. The quadruplex telegraph was Edison's first big financial success, and Menlo Park became the first institution set up with the specific purpose of producing constant technological innovation and improvement. Edison was legally attributed with most of the inventions produced there, though many employees carried out research and development under his direction.

Figure 2: *Edison's Menlo Park Laboratory, reconstructed at Greenfield Village at Henry Ford Museum in Dearborn, Michigan.*

His staff was generally told to carry out his directions in conducting research, and he drove them hard to produce results.

William Joseph Hammer, a consulting electrical engineer, started working for Edison and began his duties as a laboratory assistant in December 1879. He assisted in experiments on the telephone, phonograph, electric railway, iron ore separator, electric lighting, and other developing inventions. However, Hammer worked primarily on the incandescent electric lamp and was put in charge of tests and records on that device (see Hammer Historical Collection of Incandescent Electric Lamps). In 1880, he was appointed chief engineer of the Edison Lamp Works. In his first year, the plant under General Manager Francis Robbins Upton turned out 50,000 lamps. According to Edison, Hammer was "a pioneer of incandescent electric lighting". Frank J. Sprague, a competent mathematician and former naval officer, was recruited by Edward H. Johnson and joined the Edison organization in 1883. One of Sprague's contributions to the Edison Laboratory at Menlo Park was to expand Edison's mathematical methods. Despite the common belief that Edison did not use mathematics, analysis of his notebooks reveal that he was an astute user of mathematical analysis conducted by his assistants such as Francis Robbins Upton, for example, determining the critical parameters of his electric lighting system including lamp resistance by an analysis of Ohm's Law, Joule's Law and economics.

Nearly all of Edison's patents were utility patents, which were protected for a 17-year period and included inventions or processes that are electrical, mechanical, or chemical in nature. About a dozen were design patents, which protect an ornamental design for up to a 14-year period. As in most patents, the inventions he described were improvements over prior art. The phonograph patent, in contrast, was unprecedented as describing the first device to record and reproduce sounds.[10]

In just over a decade, Edison's Menlo Park laboratory had expanded to occupy two city blocks. Edison said he wanted the lab to have "a stock of almost every conceivable material". A newspaper article printed in 1887 reveals the seriousness of his claim, stating the lab contained "eight thousand kinds of chemicals, every kind of screw made, every size of needle, every kind of cord or wire, hair of humans, horses, hogs, cows, rabbits, goats, minx, camels ... silk in every texture, cocoons, various kinds of hoofs, shark's teeth, deer horns, tortoise shell ... cork, resin, varnish and oil, ostrich feathers, a peacock's tail, jet, amber, rubber, all ores ..." and the list goes on.

Over his desk, Edison displayed a placard with Sir Joshua Reynolds' famous quotation: "There is no expedient to which a man will not resort to avoid the real labor of thinking." This slogan was reputedly posted at several other locations throughout the facility.

With Menlo Park, Edison had created the first industrial laboratory concerned with creating knowledge and then controlling its application. Edison's name is registered on 1,093 patents.

Phonograph

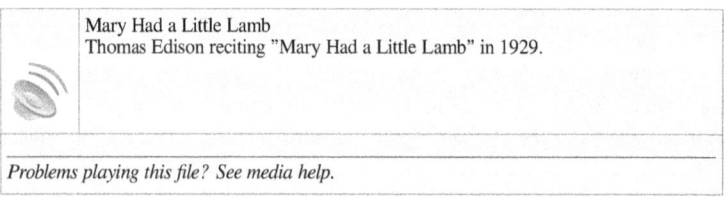

Mary Had a Little Lamb
Thomas Edison reciting "Mary Had a Little Lamb" in 1929.

Problems playing this file? See media help.

Edison began his career as an inventor in Newark, New Jersey, with the automatic repeater and his other improved telegraphic devices, but the invention that first gained him wider notice was the phonograph in 1877. This accomplishment was so unexpected by the public at large as to appear almost magical. Edison became known as "The Wizard of Menlo Park," New Jersey.

Figure 3: *Photograph of Edison with his phonograph (2nd model), taken in Mathew Brady's Washington, D.C. studio in April 1878.*

His first phonograph recorded on tinfoil around a grooved cylinder. Despite its limited sound quality and that the recordings could be played only a few times, the phonograph made Edison a celebrity. Joseph Henry, president of the National Academy of Sciences and one of the most renowned electrical scientists in the US, described Edison as "the most ingenious inventor in this country... or in any other".[11] In April 1878, Edison traveled to Washington to demonstrate the phonograph before the National Academy of Sciences, Congressmen, Senators and US President Hayes.[12] The *Washington Post* described Edison as a "genius" and his presentation as "a scene... that will live in history".[13] Although Edison obtained a patent for the phonograph in 1878,[14] he did little to develop it until Alexander Graham Bell, Chichester Bell, and Charles Tainter produced a phonograph-like device in the 1880s that used wax-coated cardboard cylinders.

Carbon telephone transmitter

In 1876, Edison began work to improve the microphone for telephones (at that time called a "transmitter") by developing a carbon microphone, which consists of two metal plates separated by granules of carbon that would change resistance with the pressure of sound waves. A steady direct current is passed between the plates through the granules and the varying resistance results in a modulation of the current, creating a varying electric current that reproduces the varying pressure of the sound wave.

Up to that point, microphones, such as the ones developed by Johann Philipp Reis and Alexander Graham Bell, worked by **generating** a weak current. The carbon microphone works by **modulating** a direct current and, subsequently, using a transformer to transfer the signal so generated to the telephone line. Edison was one of many inventors working on the problem of creating a usable microphone for telephony by having it modulate an electrical current passed through it.[15] His work was concurrent with Emile Berliner's loose-contact carbon transmitter (who lost a later patent case against Edison over the carbon transmitters invention[16]) and David Edward Hughes study and published paper on the physics of loose-contact carbon transmitters (work that Hughes did not bother to patent).[17]

Edison used the carbon microphone concept in 1877 to create an improved telephone for Western Union. In 1886, Edison found a way to improve a Bell Telephone microphone, one that used loose-contact ground carbon, with his discovery that it worked far better if the carbon was roasted. This type was put in use in 1890 and was used in all telephones along with the Bell receiver until the 1980s.

It should be noted that the frequency response of the carbon microphone is limited to a narrow frequency range (400 Hz to 4000 Hz), and the device may produce significant electrical noise.

Electric light

In 1878, Edison began working on a system of electrical illumination, something he hoped could compete with gas and oil based lighting.[18] He began by tackling the problem of creating a long-lasting incandescent lamp, something that would be needed for indoor use. Many earlier inventors had previously devised incandescent lamps, including Alessandro Volta's demonstration of a glowing wire in 1800 and inventions by Henry Woodward and Mathew Evans. Others who developed early and commercially impractical incandescent electric lamps included Humphry Davy, James Bowman Lindsay, Moses G. Farmer, William E. Sawyer, Joseph Swan, and Heinrich Göbel. Some of these early bulbs had such flaws as an extremely short life, high expense to produce, and high electric current drawn, making them difficult to apply on a large scale commercially.:[217–218] Edison realized that to connect a series of electric lights to an economically manageable size and using the necessary thickness of copper wire, he would have to develop a lamp that used a low amount of current. This lamp must have high resistance and use relatively low voltage (around 110 volts).[19]

Figure 4: *Thomas Edison's first successful light bulb model, used in public demonstration at Menlo Park, December 1879*

After many experiments, first with carbon filaments and then with platinum and other metals, Edison returned to a carbon filament. The first successful test was on October 22, 1879;:[186] it lasted 13.5 hours. Edison continued to improve this design and on November 4, 1879, filed for U.S. patent 223,898 (granted on January 27, 1880) for an electric lamp using "a carbon filament or strip coiled and connected to platina contact wires". This was the first commercially practical incandescent light.

Although the patent described several ways of creating the carbon filament including "cotton and linen thread, wood splints, papers coiled in various ways", it was not until several months after the patent was granted that Edison and his team discovered a carbonized bamboo filament that could last over 1,200 hours. The idea of using this particular raw material originated from Edison's recalling his examination of a few threads from a bamboo fishing pole while relaxing on the shore of Battle Lake in the present-day state of Wyoming, where he and other members of a scientific team had traveled so that they could clearly observe a total eclipse of the sun on July 29, 1878, from the Continental Divide.

In 1878, Edison formed the Edison Electric Light Company in New York City with several financiers, including J. P. Morgan, Spencer Trask,[20] and the members of the Vanderbilt family. Edison made the first public demonstration of

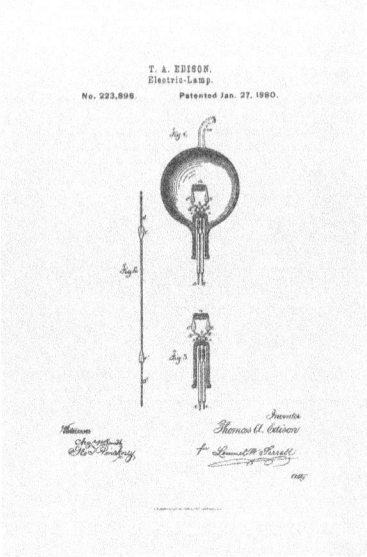

Figure 5: *U.S. Patent#223898: Electric-Lamp. Issued January 27, 1880.*

his incandescent light bulb on December 31, 1879, in Menlo Park. It was during this time that he said: "We will make electricity so cheap that only the rich will burn candles."

Henry Villard, president of the Oregon Railroad and Navigation Company, attended Edison's 1879 demonstration. Villard was impressed and requested Edison install his electric lighting system aboard Villard's company's new steamer, the *Columbia*. Although hesitant at first, Edison agreed to Villard's request. Most of the work was completed in May 1880, and the *Columbia* went to New York City, where Edison and his personnel installed *Columbia*'s new lighting system. The *Columbia* was Edison's first commercial application for his incandescent light bulb. The Edison equipment was removed from *Columbia* in 1895.[21,22,23]

Lewis Latimer joined the Edison Electric Light Company in 1884. Latimer had received a patent in January 1881 for the "Process of Manufacturing Carbons", an improved method for the production of carbon filaments for light bulbs. Latimer worked as an engineer, a draftsman and an expert witness in patent litigation on electric lights.

George Westinghouse's company bought Philip Diehl's competing induction lamp patent rights (1882) for $25,000, forcing the holders of the Edison patent

Figure 6: *The Oregon Railroad and Navigation Company's new steamship, the Columbia, was the first commercial application for Edison's incandescent light bulb in 1880.*

to charge a more reasonable rate for the use of the Edison patent rights and lowering the price of the electric lamp.[24]

On October 8, 1883, the US patent office ruled that Edison's patent was based on the work of William E. Sawyer and was, therefore, invalid. Litigation continued for nearly six years, until October 6, 1889, when a judge ruled that Edison's electric light improvement claim for "a filament of carbon of high resistance" was valid. To avoid a possible court battle with Joseph Swan, whose British patent had been awarded a year before Edison's, he and Swan formed a joint company called Ediswan to manufacture and market the invention in Britain.

Mahen Theatre in Brno (in what is now the Czech Republic), opened in 1882, and was the first public building in the world to use Edison's electric lamps. Francis Jehl, Edison's assistant in the invention of the lamp, supervised the installation. In September 2010, a sculpture of three giant light bulbs was erected in Brno, in front of the theatre.

Figure 7: *Extravagant displays of electric lights quickly became a feature of public events, as in this picture from the 1897 Tennessee Centennial Exposition.*

Electric power distribution

After devising a commercially viable electric light bulb on October 21, 1879, Edison developed an electric "utility" to compete with the existing gas light utilities.[25] On December 17, 1880, he founded the Edison Illuminating Company, and during the 1880s, he patented a system for electricity distribution. The company established the first investor-owned electric utility in 1882 on Pearl Street Station, New York City. On September 4, 1882, Edison switched on his Pearl Street generating station's electrical power distribution system, which provided 110 volts direct current (DC) to 59 customers in lower Manhattan.

In January 1882, Edison switched on the first steam-generating power station at Holborn Viaduct in London. The DC supply system provided electricity supplies to street lamps and several private dwellings within a short distance of the station. On January 19, 1883, the first standardized incandescent electric lighting system employing overhead wires began service in Roselle, New Jersey.

War of currents

As Edison expanded his direct current (DC) power delivery system, he received stiff competition from companies installing alternating current (AC) systems. From the early 1880s AC arc lighting systems for streets and large spaces had been an expanding business in the US. With the development of transformers in Europe and by Westinghouse Electric in the US in 1885–1886, it became possible to transmit AC long distances over thinner and cheaper wires, and "step down" the voltage at the destination for distribution to users. This allowed AC to be used in street lighting and in lighting for small business and domestic customers, the market Edison's patented low voltage DC incandescent lamp system was designed to supply.[26] Edison's DC empire suffered from one of its chief drawbacks: it was suitable only for the high density of customers found in large cities. Edison's DC plants could not deliver electricity to customers more than one mile from the plant, and left a patchwork of unsupplied customers between plants. Small cities and rural areas could not afford an Edison style system at all, leaving a large part of the market without electrical service. AC companies expanded into this gap.

Edison expressed views that AC was unworkable and the high voltages used were dangerous. As George Westinghouse installed his first AC systems in 1886, Thomas Edison struck out personally against his chief rival stating, *"Just as certain as death, Westinghouse will kill a customer within six months after he puts in a system of any size. He has got a new thing and it will require a great deal of experimenting to get it working practically."*[27] Many reasons have been suggested for Edison's anti-AC stance. One notion is that the inventor could not grasp the more abstract theories behind AC and was trying to avoid developing a system he did not understand. Edison also appeared to have been worried about the high voltage from misinstalled AC systems killing customers and hurting the sales of electric power systems in general.[28] Primary was the fact that Edison Electric based their design on low voltage DC and switching a standard after they had installed over 100 systems was, in Edison's mind, out of the question. By the end of 1887, Edison Electric was losing market share to Westinghouse, who had built 68 AC-based power stations to Edison's 121 DC-based stations. To make matters worse for Edison, the Thomson-Houston Electric Company of Lynn, Massachusetts (another AC-based competitor) built 22 power stations.

Parallel to expanding competition between Edison and the AC companies was rising public furor over a series of deaths in the spring of 1888 caused by pole mounted high voltage alternating current lines. This turned into a media frenzy against high voltage alternating current and the seemingly greedy and callous lighting companies that used it.[29,30] Edison took advantage of the public perception of AC as dangerous, and joined with self-styled New York anti-AC crusader Harold P. Brown in a propaganda campaign, aiding Brown in the public electrocution of animals with AC, and supported legislation to control and severely limit AC installations and voltages (to the point of making it an ineffective power delivery system) in what was now being referred to

Figure 8: *Thomas A. Edison Industries Exhibit, Primary Battery section, 1915*

as a "battle of currents". The development of the electric chair was used in an attempt to portray AC as having a greater lethal potential than DC and smear Westinghouse at the same time via Edison colluding with Brown and Westinghouse's chief AC rival, the Thomson-Houston Electric Company, to make sure the first electric chair was powered by a Westinghouse AC generator.

Thomas Edison's staunch anti-AC tactics were not sitting well with his own stockholders. By the early 1890s, Edison's company was generating much smaller profits than its AC rivals, and the War of Currents would come to an end in 1892 with Edison forced out of controlling his own company. That year, the financier J.P. Morgan engineered a merger of Edison General Electric with Thomson-Houston that put the board of Thomson-Houston in charge of the new company called General Electric. General Electric now controlled three-quarters of the US electrical business and would compete with Westinghouse for the AC market.[31,32]

West Orange and Fort Myers (1886–1931)

Edison moved from Menlo Park after the death of his first wife, Mary, in 1884, and purchased a home known as "Glenmont" in 1886 as a wedding gift for his second wife, Mina, in Llewellyn Park in West Orange, New Jersey. In 1885, Thomas Edison bought property in Fort Myers, Florida, and built what was later called Seminole Lodge as a winter retreat. Edison and Mina spent many winters at their home in Fort Myers, and Edison tried to find a domestic source of natural rubber.

Due to the security concerns around World War I, Edison suggested forming a science and industry committee to provide advice and research to the US military, and he headed the Naval Consulting Board in 1915.

Edison's work on rubber took place largely at his research laboratory in Fort Myers, which has been designated as a National Historic Chemical Landmark. The laboratory was built after Thomas Edison, Henry Ford, and Harvey Firestone pulled together $75,000 to form the Edison Botanical Research Corporation. Initially, only Ford and Firestone were to contribute funds to the project while Edison did all the research. Edison, however, wished to contribute $25,000 as well. After testing over 17,000 plant species, Edison decided on *Solidago leavenworthii*, also known as Leavenworth's Goldenrod. The plant, which normally grows roughly 3–4 feet tall with a 5% latex yield, was adapted by Edison through cross-breeding to produce plants twice the size and with a latex yield of 12%.[33]

Other inventions and projects

Fluoroscopy

Edison is credited with designing and producing the first commercially available fluoroscope, a machine that uses X-rays to take radiographs. Until Edison discovered that calcium tungstate fluoroscopy screens produced brighter images than the barium platinocyanide screens originally used by Wilhelm Röntgen, the technology was capable of producing only very faint images.

The fundamental design of Edison's fluoroscope is still in use today, although Edison abandoned the project after nearly losing his own eyesight and seriously injuring his assistant, Clarence Dally. Dally made himself an enthusiastic human guinea pig for the fluoroscopy project and was exposed to a poisonous dose of radiation. He later died of injuries related to the exposure. In 1903, a shaken Edison said: "Don't talk to me about X-rays, I am afraid of them."[34]

Telegraph improvements

The key to Edison's fortunes was telegraphy. With knowledge gained from years of working as a telegraph operator, he learned the basics of electricity. This allowed him to make his early fortune with the stock ticker, the first electricity-based broadcast system. On August 9, 1892, Edison received a patent for a two-way telegraph.

Figure 9: *The June 1894 Leonard–Cushing bout. Each of the six one-minute rounds recorded by the Kinetoscope was made available to exhibitors for $22.50.*[35] *Customers who watched the final round saw Leonard score a knockdown.*

Motion pictures

Edison was also granted a patent for the motion picture camera or "Kinetograph". He did the electromechanical design while his employee W. K. L. Dickson, a photographer, worked on the photographic and optical development. Much of the credit for the invention belongs to Dickson. In 1891, Thomas Edison built a Kinetoscope or peep-hole viewer. This device was installed in penny arcades, where people could watch short, simple films. The kinetograph and kinetoscope were both first publicly exhibited May 20, 1891.

In April 1896, Thomas Armat's Vitascope, manufactured by the Edison factory and marketed in Edison's name, was used to project motion pictures in public screenings in New York City. Later, he exhibited motion pictures with voice soundtrack on cylinder recordings, mechanically synchronized with the film.

Officially the kinetoscope entered Europe when the rich American Businessman Irving T. Bush (1869–1948) bought from the Continental Commerce Company of Frank Z. Maguire and Joseph D. Baucus a dozen machines. Bush placed from October 17, 1894, the first kinetoscopes in London. At the same time, the French company Kinétoscope Edison Michel et Alexis Werner bought these machines for the market in France. In the last three months of 1894, the Continental Commerce Company sold hundreds of kinetoscopes in Europe (i.e. the Netherlands and Italy). In Germany and in Austria-Hungary, the kinetoscope was introduced by the Deutsche-österreichische-Edison-Kinetoscop Gesellschaft, founded by the Ludwig Stollwerck of the Schokoladen-Süsswarenfabrik Stollwerck & Co of Cologne.

The first kinetoscopes arrived in Belgium at the Fairs in early 1895. The Edison's Kinétoscope Français, a Belgian company, was founded in Brussels on January 15, 1895, with the rights to sell the kinetoscopes in Monaco, France and the French colonies. The main investors in this company were Belgian industrialists.

On May 14, 1895, the Edison's Kinétoscope Belge was founded in Brussels. The businessman Ladislas-Victor Lewitzki, living in London but active in Belgium and France, took the initiative in starting this business. He had contacts with Leon Gaumont and the American Mutoscope and Biograph Co. In 1898, he also became a shareholder of the Biograph and Mutoscope Company for France.

Edison's film studio made close to 1,200 films. The majority of the productions were short films showing everything from acrobats to parades to fire calls including titles such as *Fred Ott's Sneeze* (1894), *The Kiss* (1896), *The Great Train Robbery* (1903), *Alice's Adventures in Wonderland* (1910), and the first *Frankenstein* film in 1910. In 1903, when the owners of Luna Park, Coney Island announced they would execute Topsy the elephant by strangulation, poisoning, and electrocution (with the electrocution part ultimately killing the elephant), Edison Manufacturing sent a crew to film it, releasing it that same year with the title *Electrocuting an Elephant*.

As the film business expanded, competing exhibitors routinely copied and exhibited each other's films.[36] To better protect the copyrights on his films, Edison deposited prints of them on long strips of photographic paper with the U.S. copyright office. Many of these paper prints survived longer and in better condition than the actual films of that era.[37]

In 1908, Edison started the Motion Picture Patents Company, which was a conglomerate of nine major film studios (commonly known as the Edison Trust). Thomas Edison was the first honorary fellow of the Acoustical Society of America, which was founded in 1929.

Edison said his favorite movie was *The Birth of a Nation*. He thought that talkies had "spoiled everything" for him. "There isn't any good acting on the screen. They concentrate on the voice now and have forgotten how to act. I can sense it more than you because I am deaf."[38] His favorite stars were Mary Pickford and Clara Bow.[39]

Figure 10: *A Day with Thomas Edison (1922)*

Mining

Starting in the late 1870s, Thomas Edison became interested and involved with mining. High-grade iron ore was scarce on the east coast of the United States and Edison tried to mine low-grade ore. Edison developed a process using rollers and crushers that could pulverize rocks up to 10 tons. The dust was then sent between three giant magnets that would pull the iron ore from the dust. Despite the failure of his mining company, the Edison Ore Milling Company, Edison used some of the materials and equipment to produce cement.

In 1901, Edison visited an industrial exhibition in the Sudbury area in Ontario, Canada and thought nickel and cobalt deposits there could be used in his production of electrical equipment. He returned as a mining prospector and is credited with the original discovery of the Falconbridge ore body. His attempts to mine the ore body were not successful, and he abandoned his mining claim in 1903. A street in Falconbridge, as well as the Edison Building, which served as the head office of Falconbridge Mines, are named for him.

Figure 11: *Share of the Edison Storage Battery Company, issued 19. October 1903*

Battery

The Edison Storage Battery Company was founded in 1901. With this company, Edison exploited his invention of the accumulator. In 1904, 450 people already worked for the company. The first accumulators were produced for electric cars, but there were several defects. Several customers complained about the products. When the capital of the company was spent, Edison paid for the company with his private money. Edison did not demonstrate a mature product until 1910: a nickel-iron-battery with lye as the electrolyte.

Rubber

Edison became concerned with America's reliance on foreign supply of rubber and was determined to find a native supply of rubber. He joined Harvey Firestone and Henry Ford (each contributing $25,000) to create the Edison Botanic Research Corp. in 1927 and constructed a laboratory in Fort Myers, Florida the following year. Edison did the majority of the research and planting, sending results and sample rubber residues to his West Orange Lab. Edison employed a two-part Acid-base extraction, to derive latex from the plant material after it was dried and crushed to a powder. After testing 17,000 plant samples, he eventually found an adequate source in the Goldenrod plant.

Figure 12: *From left to right: Henry Ford, Thomas Edison, and Harvey Firestone, the three partners of the Edison Botanic Research Corporation.*

Chemicals

At the start of World War I, the American chemical industry was primitive. Most chemicals were imported from Europe. The outbreak of war in August, 1914, resulted in an immediate shortage of imported chemicals. One of particular importance to Edison was phenol, which was used to make phonograph records–presumably as phenolic resins of the Bakelite type.

At the time, phenol came from coal as a by-product of coke oven gases or manufactured gas for gaslighting. Phenol could be nitrated to picric acid and converted to ammonium picrate, a shock resistant high explosive suitable for use in artillery shells. The best telling of the phenol story is found in "The Aspirin Wars."[40] Most phenol had been imported from Britain, but with war, Parliament blocked exports and diverted most to production of ammonium picrate. Britain also blockaded supplies from Germany.

Edison responded by undertaking production of phenol at his Silver Lake, NJ, facility using processes developed by his chemists.[41] He built two plants with a capacity of six tons of phenol per day. Production began the first week of September, one month after hostilities began in Europe. He built two plants to produce raw material benzene at Johnstown, PA and Bessemer, AL, replacing supplies previously from Germany. Edison also manufactured aniline dyes, which previously had been supplied by the German dye trust. Other wartime products include xylene, p-phenylenediamine, shellac, and pyrax. Wartime shortages made these ventures profitable. In 1915, his production capacity was fully committed by midyear.

Phenol was a critical material because two derivatives were in high growth phases. Bakelite, the original thermoset plastic, had been invented in 1909. Aspirin, too was a phenol derivative. Invented in 1899 had become a block buster drug. Bayer had acquired a plant to manufacture in the US in Rensselaer, NY, but struggled to find phenol to keep their plant running during the war. Edison was able to oblige.

Bayer relied on Chemische Fabrik von Heyden, in Piscataway, NJ, to convert phenol to salicylic acid, which they converted to aspirin. (See Great Phenol plot.) It is said that German companies bought up supplies of phenol to block production of ammonium picrate. Edison preferred not to sell phenol for military uses. He sold his surplus to Bayer, who had it converted to salicylic acid by Heyden, some of which was exported.

Final years and death

Final years

Henry Ford, the automobile magnate, later lived a few hundred feet away from Edison at his winter retreat in Fort Myers. Ford once worked as an engineer for the Edison Illuminating Company of Detroit and met Edison at a convention of affiliated Edison illuminating companies in Brooklyn, NY in 1896. Edison was impressed with Ford's internal combustion engine automobile and encouraged its developments. They were friends until Edison's death. Edison and Ford undertook annual motor camping trips from 1914 to 1924. Harvey Firestone and John Burroughs also participated.

In 1928, Edison joined the Fort Myers Civitan Club. He believed strongly in the organization, writing that "The Civitan Club is doing things—big things—for the community, state, and nation, and I certainly consider it an honor to be numbered in its ranks." He was an active member in the club until his death, sometimes bringing Henry Ford to the club's meetings.

Edison was active in business right up to the end. Just months before his death, the Lackawanna Railroad inaugurated suburban electric train service from Hoboken to Montclair, Dover, and Gladstone, New Jersey. Electrical transmission for this service was by means of an overhead catenary system using direct current, which Edison had championed. Despite his frail condition,

Figure 13: *Henry Ford, Thomas Edison, and Harvey Firestone, respectively. Ft. Myers, Florida, February 11, 1929*

Edison was at the throttle of the first electric MU (Multiple-Unit) train to depart Lackawanna Terminal in Hoboken in September 1930, driving the train the first mile through Hoboken yard on its way to South Orange.

This fleet of cars would serve commuters in northern New Jersey for the next 54 years until their retirement in 1984. A plaque commemorating Edison's inaugural ride can be seen today in the waiting room of Lackawanna Terminal in Hoboken, which is presently operated by New Jersey Transit.

Edison was said to have been influenced by a popular fad diet in his last few years; "the only liquid he consumed was a pint of milk every three hours". He is reported to have believed this diet would restore his health. However, this tale is doubtful. In 1930, the year before Edison died, Mina said in an interview about him, "correct eating is one of his greatest hobbies." She also said that during one of his periodic "great scientific adventures", Edison would be up at 7:00, have breakfast at 8:00, and be rarely home for lunch or dinner, implying that he continued to have all three.

Edison became the owner of his Milan, Ohio, birthplace in 1906. On his last visit, in 1923, he was reportedly shocked to find his old home still lit by lamps and candles.Wikipedia:Citation needed

Death

Edison died of complications of diabetes on October 18, 1931, in his home, "Glenmont" in Llewellyn Park in West Orange, New Jersey, which he had purchased in 1886 as a wedding gift for Mina. Rev. Stephen J. Herben officiated at the funeral; Edison is buried behind the home.

Edison's last breath is reportedly contained in a test tube at The Henry Ford museum near Detroit. Ford reportedly convinced Charles Edison to seal a test tube of air in the inventor's room shortly after his death, as a memento.[42] A plaster death mask and casts of Edison's hands were also made.[43] Mina died in 1947.

Marriages and children

On December 25, 1871, at the age of twenty-four, Edison married 16-year-old Mary Stilwell (1855–1884), whom he had met two months earlier; she was an employee at one of his shops. They had three children:

- Marion Estelle Edison (1873–1965), nicknamed "Dot"[44]
- Thomas Alva Edison Jr. (1876–1935), nicknamed "Dash"[45]
- William Leslie Edison (1878–1937) Inventor, graduate of the Sheffield Scientific School at Yale, 1900.

Mary Edison died at age 29 on August 9, 1884, of unknown causes: possibly from a brain tumor[46] or a morphine overdose. Doctors frequently prescribed morphine to women in those years to treat a variety of causes, and researchers believe that her symptoms could have been from morphine poisoning.[47]

Edison generally preferred spending time in the laboratory to being with his family.

On February 24, 1886, at the age of thirty-nine, Edison married the 20-year-old Mina Miller (1865–1947) in Akron, Ohio. She was the daughter of the inventor Lewis Miller, co-founder of the Chautauqua Institution, and a benefactor of Methodist charities. They also had three children together:

- Madeleine Edison (1888–1979), who married John Eyre Sloane.
- Charles Edison (1890–1969), Governor of New Jersey (1941–1944), who took over his father's company and experimental laboratories upon his father's death.
- Theodore Miller Edison (1898–1992), (MIT Physics 1923), credited with more than 80 patents.

Figure 14: *Mina Miller Edison in 1906*

Mina outlived Thomas Edison, dying on August 24, 1947.

Wanting to be an inventor, but not having much of an aptitude for it, Thomas Edison's son, Thomas Alva Edison Jr.. became a problem for his father and his father's business. Starting in the 1890s, Thomas Jr. became involved in snake oil products and shady and fraudulent enterprises producing products being sold to the public as *"The Latest Edison Discovery"*. The situation became so bad that Thomas Sr. had to take his son to court to stop the practices, finally agreeing to pay Thomas Jr. an allowance of $35.00 (equivalent to $953 in 2017[9]<templatestyles src="Module:Citation/CS1/styles.css"></templatestyles>) per week, in exchange for not using the Edison name; the son began using aliases, such as Burton Willard. Thomas Jr., suffering from alcoholism, depression and ill health, worked at several menial jobs, but by 1931 (towards the end of his life) he would obtain a role in the Edison company, thanks to the intervention of his brother.

Views

On politics, religion, and metaphysics

Historian Paul Israel has characterized Edison as a "freethinker". Edison was heavily influenced by Thomas Paine's *The Age of Reason*. Edison defended Paine's "scientific deism", saying, "He has been called an atheist, but atheist he was not. Paine believed in a supreme intelligence, as representing the idea which other men often express by the name of deity." In 1878, Edison joined the Theosophical Society in New Jersey, but according to its founder, H. P. Blavatsky, he was not a very active member. In an October 2, 1910, interview in the *New York Times Magazine*, Edison stated:

> *Nature is what we know. We do not know the gods of religions. And nature is not kind, or merciful, or loving. If God made me — the fabled God of the three qualities of which I spoke: mercy, kindness, love — He also made the fish I catch and eat. And where do His mercy, kindness, and love for that fish come in? No; nature made us — nature did it all — not the gods of the religions.*

Edison was accused of being an atheist for those remarks, and although he did not allow himself to be drawn into the controversy publicly, he clarified himself in a private letter:

> *You have misunderstood the whole article, because you jumped to the conclusion that it denies the existence of God. There is no such denial, what you call God I call Nature, the Supreme intelligence that rules matter. All the article states is that it is doubtful in my opinion if our intelligence or soul or whatever one may call it lives hereafter as an entity or disperses back again from whence it came, scattered amongst the cells of which we are made.*

He also stated, "I do not believe in the God of the theologians; but that there is a Supreme Intelligence I do not doubt."[48]

Nonviolence was key to Edison's moral views, and when asked to serve as a naval consultant for World War I, he specified he would work only on defensive weapons and later noted, "I am proud of the fact that I never invented weapons to kill." Edison's philosophy of nonviolence extended to animals as well, about which he stated: "Nonviolence leads to the highest ethics, which is the goal of all evolution. Until we stop harming all other living beings, we are still savages."[49] He was a vegetarian but not a vegan in actual practice, at least near the end of his life.

In 1920, Edison set off a media sensation when he told B. C. Forbes of *American Magazine* that he was working on a "spirit phone" to allow communication with the dead, a story which other newspapers and magazines repeated. Edison later disclaimed the idea, telling the New York Times in 1926 that "I really had nothing to tell him, but I hated to disappoint him so I thought up this story about communicating with spirits, but it was all a joke."

On the monetary system

Thomas Edison was an advocate for monetary reform in the United States. He was ardently opposed to the gold standard and debt-based money. Famously, he was quoted in the New York Times stating "Gold is a relic of Julius Caesar, and interest is an invention of Satan."

In the same article, he expounded upon the absurdity of a monetary system in which the taxpayer of the United States, in need of a loan, can be compelled to pay in return perhaps double the principal, or even greater sums, due to interest. His basic point was that, if the Government can produce debt-based money, it could equally as well produce money that was a credit to the taxpayer.

He thought at length about the subject of money in 1921 and 1922. In May 1922, he published a proposal, entitled "A Proposed Amendment to the Federal Reserve Banking System".[50] In it, he detailed an explanation of a commodity-backed currency, in which the Federal Reserve would issue interest-free currency to farmers, based on the value of commodities they produced. During a publicity tour that he took with friend and fellow inventor, Henry Ford, he spoke publicly about his desire for monetary reform. For insight, he corresponded with prominent academic and banking professionals. In the end, however, Edison's proposals failed to find support and were eventually abandoned.

Awards

The President of the Third French Republic, Jules Grévy, on the recommendation of his Minister of Foreign Affairs, Jules Barthélemy-Saint-Hilaire, and with the presentations of the Minister of Posts and Telegraphs, Louis Cochery, designated Edison with the *distinction* of an Officer of the Legion of Honour (Légion d'honneur) by decree on November 10, 1881;[51] Edison was also named a Chevalier in the Legion in 1879, and a Commander in 1889.

In 1887, Edison won the Matteucci Medal. In 1890, he was elected a member of the Royal Swedish Academy of Sciences.

The Philadelphia City Council named Edison the recipient of the John Scott Medal in 1889.

In 1899, Edison was awarded the Edward Longstreth Medal of The Franklin Institute.

Figure 15: *Portrait of Edison by Abraham Archibald Anderson (1890), National Portrait Gallery*

He was named an Honorable Consulting Engineer at the Louisiana Purchase Exposition World's fair in 1904.

In 1908, Edison received the American Association of Engineering Societies John Fritz Medal.

In 1915, Edison was awarded Franklin Medal of The Franklin Institute for discoveries contributing to the foundation of industries and the well-being of the human race.

In 1920, the United States Navy department awarded him the Navy Distinguished Service Medal.

In 1923, the American Institute of Electrical Engineers created the Edison Medal and he was its first recipient.

In 1927, he was granted membership in the National Academy of Sciences.

On May 29, 1928, Edison received the Congressional Gold Medal.

In 1983, the United States Congress, pursuant to Senate Joint Resolution 140 (Public Law 97—198), designated February 11, Edison's birthday, as National Inventor's Day.

Figure 16: *Thomas Edison commemorative stamp, issued on the 100th anniversary of his birth in 1947*

Life magazine (USA), in a special double issue in 1997, placed Edison first in the list of the "100 Most Important People in the Last 1000 Years", noting that the light bulb he promoted "lit up the world". In the 2005 television series *The Greatest American*, he was voted by viewers as the fifteenth greatest.

In 2008, Edison was inducted in the New Jersey Hall of Fame.

In 2010, Edison was honored with a Technical Grammy Award.

In 2011, Edison was inducted into the Entrepreneur Walk of Fame and named a Great Floridian by the Florida Governor and Cabinet.

Tributes

Places and people named for Edison

Several places have been named after Edison, most notably the town of Edison, New Jersey. Thomas Edison State University, nationally known for adult learners, is in Trenton, New Jersey. Two community colleges are named for him: Edison State College (now Florida SouthWestern State College) in Fort Myers, Florida, and Edison Community College in Piqua, Ohio. There are numerous high schools named after Edison (see Edison High School) and other

Figure 17: *Statue of young Thomas Edison by the railroad tracks in Port Huron, Michigan.*

schools including Thomas A. Edison Middle School. Footballer Pelé's father originally named him Edson, as a tribute to the inventor of the light bulb, but the name was incorrectly listed on his birth certificate as "Edison".

The small town of Alva just east of Fort Myers took Edison's middle name.

In 1883, the City Hotel in Sunbury, Pennsylvania was the first building to be lit with Edison's three-wire system. The hotel was renamed The Hotel Edison upon Edison's return to the city on 1922.

Lake Thomas A Edison in California was named after Edison to mark the 75th anniversary of the incandescent light bulb.

Edison was on hand to turn on the lights at the Hotel Edison in New York City when it opened in 1931.

Three bridges around the United States have been named in Edison's honor: the Edison Bridge in New Jersey, the Edison Bridge in Florida, and the Edison Bridge in Ohio.

In space, his name is commemorated in asteroid 742 Edisona.

Museums and memorials

In West Orange, New Jersey, the 13.5 acres (5.5 hectares) Glenmont estate is maintained and operated by the National Park Service as the Edison National Historic Site, as is his nearby laboratory and workshops including the reconstructed "Black Maria"—the world's first movie studio. The Thomas Alva Edison Memorial Tower and Museum is in the town of Edison, New Jersey.[52] In Beaumont, Texas, there is an Edison Museum, though Edison never visited there. The Port Huron Museum, in Port Huron, Michigan, restored the original depot that Thomas Edison worked out of as a young news butcher. The depot has been named the Thomas Edison Depot Museum.[53] The town has many Edison historical landmarks, including the graves of Edison's parents, and a monument along the St. Clair River. Edison's influence can be seen throughout this city of 32,000.

In Detroit, the Edison Memorial Fountain in Grand Circus Park was created to honor his achievements. The limestone fountain was dedicated October 21, 1929, the fiftieth anniversary of the creation of the lightbulb.[54] On the same night, The Edison Institute was dedicated in nearby Dearborn.

He was inducted into the Automotive Hall of Fame in 1969.Wikipedia:Citation needed

A bronze statue of Edison was placed in the National Statuary Hall Collection at the United States Capitol in 2016, with the formal dedication ceremony held on September 20 of that year. The Edison statue replaced one of 19th-century state governor William Allen that had been one of Ohio's two allowed contributions to the collection.

Companies bearing Edison's name

- Edison General Electric, merged with Thomson-Houston Electric Company to form General Electric
- Commonwealth Edison, now part of Exelon
- Consolidated Edison
- Edison International
- Detroit Edison, a unit of DTE Energy
- Edison S.p.A., a unit of Italenergia
- Trade association the Edison Electric Institute, a lobbying and research group for investor-owned utilities in the United States
- Edison Ore-Milling Company
- Edison Portland Cement Company
- Ohio Edison (merged with Centerior in 1997 to form First Energy)
- Southern California Edison

Figure 18: *Edison in 1915*

Awards named in honor of Edison

The Edison Medal was created on February 11, 1904, by a group of Edison's friends and associates. Four years later the American Institute of Electrical Engineers (AIEE), later IEEE, entered into an agreement with the group to present the medal as its highest award. The first medal was presented in 1909 to Elihu Thomson. It is the oldest award in the area of electrical and electronics engineering, and is presented annually "for a career of meritorious achievement in electrical science, electrical engineering or the electrical arts."

In the Netherlands, the major music awards are named the Edison Award after him. The award is an annual Dutch music prize, awarded for outstanding achievements in the music industry, and is one of the oldest music awards in the world, having been presented since 1960.

The American Society of Mechanical Engineers concedes the Thomas A. Edison Patent Award to individual patents since 2000.

Other items named after Edison

The United States Navy named the USS *Edison* (DD-439), a Gleaves class destroyer, in his honor in 1940. The ship was decommissioned a few months after the end of World War II. In 1962, the Navy commissioned USS *Thomas A. Edison* (SSBN-610), a fleet ballistic missile nuclear-powered submarine.

In popular culture

Thomas Edison has appeared in popular culture as a character in novels, films, comics and video games. His prolific inventing helped make him an icon and he has made appearances in popular culture during his lifetime down to the present day. Edison is also portrayed in popular culture as an adversary of Nikola Tesla.

"Camping with Henry and Tom", a fictional play based on Edison's camping trips with Henry Ford, written by Mark St.Gemain. First presented at Lucille Lortel Theatre, New York, February 20, 1995.Wikipedia:Citation needed

On February 11, 2011, on what would have been Thomas Edison's 164th birthday, Google's homepage featured an animated Google Doodle commemorating his many inventions. When the cursor was hovered over the doodle, a series of mechanisms seemed to move, causing a lightbulb to glow.

List of people who worked for Edison

The following is a list of people who worked for Thomas Edison in his laboratories at Menlo Park or West Orange or at the subsidiary electrical businesses that he supervised.

- Edward Goodrich Acheson – chemist, worked at Menlo Park 1880–1884
- William Symes Andrews – started at the Menlo Park machine shop 1879
- Charles Batchelor – "chief experimental assistant"
- John I. Beggs – manager of Edison Illuminating Company in New York, 1886
- William Kennedy Dickson – joined Menlo Park in 1823, worked on the motion picture camera
- Justus B. Entz – joined Edison Machine Works in 1887
- Reginald Fessenden – worked at the Edison Machine Works in 1886
- Henry Ford – engineer Edison Illuminating Company Detroit, Michigan, 1891–1899
- William Joseph Hammer – started as laboratory assistant Menlo Park in 1879
- Miller Reese Hutchison – inventor of hearing aid

- Edward Hibberd Johnson – started in 1909, chief engineer at West Orange laboratory 1912–1918
- Samuel Insull – started in 1881, rose to become VP of General Electric (1892) then President of Chicago Edison
- Kunihiko Iwadare – joined Edison Machine Works in 1887
- Francis Jehl – laboratory assistant Menlo Park 1879–1882
- Arthur E. Kennelly – engineer, experimentalist at West Orange laboratory 1887–1894
- John Kruesi – started 1872, was head machinist, at Newark, Menlo Park, Edison Machine Works
- Lewis Howard Latimer – hired 1884 as a draftsman, continued working for General Electric
- John W. Lieb – worked at the Edison Machine Works in 1881
- Thomas Commerford Martin – electrical engineer, worked at Menlo Park 1877–1879
- George F. Morrison – started at Edison Lamp Works 1882
- Edwin Stanton Porter – joined the Edison Manufacturing Company 1899
- Frank J. Sprague – Joined Menlo Park 1883, became known as the "Father of Electric Traction".
- Nikola Tesla – electrical engineer and inventor, worked at the Edison Machine Works in 1884
- Francis Robbins Upton – mathematician/physicist, joined Menlo Park 1878

Bibliography

External video

Booknotes interview with Neil Baldwin on *Edison: Inventing the Century*, March 19, 1995[55], C-SPAN

Booknotes interview with Jill Jonnes on *Empires of Light*, October 26, 2003[56], C-SPAN

<templatestyles src="Template:Refbegin/styles.css" />

- Albion, Michele Wehrwein. (2008). *The Florida Life of Thomas Edison*. Gainesville: University Press of Florida. ISBN 978-0-8130-3259-7.<templatestyles src="Module:Citation/CS1/styles.css"></templatestyles>
- Adams, Glen J. (2004). *The Search for Thomas Edison's Boyhood Home*. ISBN 978-1-4116-1361-4.<templatestyles src="Module:Citation/CS1/styles.css"></templatestyles>

- Angel, Ernst (1926). *Edison. Sein Leben und Erfinden*. Berlin: Ernst Angel Verlag.
- Baldwin, Neil (2001). *Edison: Inventing the Century*. University of Chicago Press. ISBN 978-0-226-03571-0.
- Clark, Ronald William (1977). *Edison: The man who made the future*. London: Macdonald & Jane's: Macdonald and Jane's. ISBN 978-0-354-04093-8.
- Conot, Robert (1979). *A Streak of Luck*. New York: Seaview Books. ISBN 978-0-87223-521-2.
- Davis, L. J. (1998). *Fleet Fire: Thomas Edison and the Pioneers of the Electric Revolution*. New York: Doubleday. ISBN 978-0-385-47927-1.
- Essig, Mark (2004). *Edison and the Electric Chair*. Stroud: Sutton. ISBN 978-0-7509-3680-4.
- Essig, Mark (2003). *Edison & the Electric Chair: A Story of Light and Death*. New York: Walker & Company. ISBN 978-0-8027-1406-0.
- Israel, Paul (1998). *Edison: A Life of Invention*. New York: Wiley. ISBN 978-0-471-52942-2.
- Jonnes, Jill (2003). *Empires of Light: Edison, Tesla, Westinghouse, and the Race to Electrify the World*. New York: Random House. ISBN 978-0-375-50739-7.
- Josephson, Matthew (1959). *Edison*. McGraw Hill. ISBN 978-0-07-033046-7.
- Koenigsberg, Allen (1987). *Edison Cylinder Records, 1889–1912*. APM Press. ISBN 0-937612-07-3.
- Pretzer, William S. (ed). (1989). *Working at Inventing: Thomas A. Edison and the Menlo Park Experience*. Dearborn, Michigan: Henry Ford Museum & Greenfield Village. ISBN 978-0-933728-33-2.
- Stross, Randall E. (2007). *The Wizard of Menlo*

Park: How Thomas Alva Edison Invented the Modern World. Crown. ISBN 1-4000-4762-5.<templatestyles src="Module:Citation/CS1/styles.css"></templatestyles>

External links

Wikimedia Commons has media related to *Thomas Edison*.

Wikiquote has quotations related to: *Thomas Edison*

Wikisourcehas original text related to this article:
Author:Thomas Edison

Museums

- Menlo Park Museum and Edison Memorial Tower[57]
- Thomas Edison National Historical Park[58] (National Park Service)
- Edison exhibit and Menlo Park Laboratory at Henry Ford Museum[59]
- Edison Museum[60]
- Edison Depot Museum[61]
- Edison Birthplace Museum[62]
- Thomas Edison House[63]

Information and media

- Thomas Edison[64] at *Encyclopædia Britannica*
- Thomas Edison[65] on *In Our Time* at the BBC
- Interview with Thomas Edison in 1931[66]
- The Diary of Thomas Edison[67]
- Works by Thomas Edison[68] at Project Gutenberg
- Works by or about Thomas Edison[69] at Internet Archive
- Edison's patent application for the light bulb[70] at the National Archives.
- Thomas Edison[71] on IMDb
- "January 4, 1903: Edison Fries an Elephant to Prove His Point"[72] – *Wired* article about Edison's "macabre form of a series of animal electrocutions using AC."
- "The Invention Factory: Thomas Edison's Laboratories"[73] National Park Service (NPS)
- Thomas Edison Personal Manuscripts and Letters[74]

- *Edison, His Life and Inventions* at Project Gutenberg by Frank Lewis Dyer and Thomas Commerford Martin.
- The short film *Story of Thomas Alva Edison*[75] is available for free download at the Internet Archive
- Edison Papers[76] Rutgers.
- Edisonian Museum Antique Electrics[77]
- Edison Innovation Foundation[78] – Non-profit foundation supporting the legacy of Thomas Edison.
- Thomas Alva Edison[79] at Find a Grave
- The Illustrious Vagabonds[80] Henry Ford Heritage Association
- "The World's Greatest Inventor"[81] October 1931, *Popular Mechanics*. Detailed, illustrated article.
- 14 minutes "instructional" film with fictional elements The boyhood of Thomas Edison[82] from 1964, produced by Coronet, published by archive.org
- "A Day with Thomas A. Edison" Video[83] on YouTube – 1922 – A rare documentary silent film
- "Edison's Miracle of Light"[84] PBS – *American Experience*. Premiered January 2015.
- Newspaper clippings about Thomas Edison[85] in the 20th Century Press Archives of the German National Library of Economics (ZBW)

Awards and achievements		
Preceded by **Leon Trotsky**	Cover of *Time* magazine	Succeeded by **Richard Swann Lull**

Appendix
References

[1] Thomas Edison's Inventive Life; by Joyce Bedi http://invention.si.edu/thomas-edisons-inventive-life Retrieved March 31, 2018

[2] "Edison" by Matthew Josephson. McGraw Hill, New York, 1959,

[3] "Edison: Inventing the Century" by Neil Baldwin, University of Chicago Press, 2001,

[4] Josephson, p 18

[5] Baldwin, page 37

[6] Baldwin, pages 40–41

[7] //www.google.com/patents/US90646

[8] The Edison Papers http://edison.rutgers.edu/vote.htm, Rutgers University. Retrieved March 20, 2007.

[9] Federal Reserve Bank of Minneapolis Community Development Project. "Consumer Price Index (estimate) 1800–" https://www.minneapolisfed.org/community/financial-and-economic-education/cpi-calculator-information/consumer-price-index-1800. Federal Reserve Bank of Minneapolis. Retrieved January 2, 2018.

[10] Evans, Harold, "They Made America." Little, Brown and Company, New York, 2004. p. 152.

[11] Edison, Thomas A. 1989. *Menlo Park: The early years, April 1876 – December 1877*. Edited by P. B. Israel, K. A. Nier and L. Carlat. Vol. 3, The papers of Thomas A Edison. Baltimore: Johns Hopkins University Press. Doc. 1117

[12] Baldwin, Neil. 2001. *Edison: Inventing the century*. Chicago: University of Chicago Press. pp.97–98

[13] Washington Post. 1878. *Genius before science*. Washington Post, April 19.

[14] Edison, Thomas A. 1877. *Telephones or speaking-telegraphs*. US patent 203,018 filed December 13, 1877, and issued April 30, 1878.

[15] Adrian Hope, 100 Years of Microphone, New Scientist May 11, 1978 Vol. 78, No. 1102, page 378 ISSN 0262-4079

[16] *IEEE Global History Network: Carbon Transmitter*. New Brunswick, NJ: IEEE History Center

[17] *David Edward Hughes: Concertinist and Inventor*

[18] Howard B. Rockman, Intellectual Property Law for Engineers and Scientists, John Wiley & Sons – 2004, page 131

[19] Jill Jonnes, Empires Of Light: Edison, Tesla, Westinghouse, And The Race To Electrify The World, Random House – 2004, page 60

[20] "Handbook of Research on Venture Capital". Colin Mason. Edward Elgar Publishing. January 1, 2012. pg 17

[21] Jehl, Francis Menlo Park reminiscences : written in Edison's restored Menlo Park laboratory https://books.google.com/books?id=OkL1Smk4uiAC&pg=PA563&dq=SS+Columbia+ (1880), Henry Ford Museum and Greenfield Village, Whitefish, Mass, Kessinger Publishing, July 1, 2002, page 564

[22] Dalton, Anthony A long, dangerous coastline: shipwreck tales from Alaska to California https://books.google.com/books?id=LOQ67VeU3WwC&pg=PA63&dq=SS+Columbia+(1880) Heritage House Publishing Company, February 1, 2011 – 128 pages

[23] Swann, p. 242.

[24] "Diehl's Lamp Hit Edison Monopoly," Elizabeth Daily Journal, Friday Evening, October 25, 1929

[25] Ahmad Faruqui, Kelly Eakin, Pricing in Competitive Electricity Markets, Springer Science & Business Media – 2000, page 67

[26] Jill Jonnes, Empires Of Light: Edison, Tesla, Westinghouse, And The Race To Electrify The World, Random House – 2004, pages 54–60

[27] Maury Klein, The Power Makers: Steam, Electricity, and the Men Who Invented Modern America, Bloomsbury Publishing USA – 2008, page 257

[28] Empires Of Light: Edison, Tesla, Westinghouse, And The Race To Electrify The By Jill Jonnes page 146
[29] Jill Jonnes, Empires Of Light: Edison, Tesla, Westinghouse, And The Race To Electrify The World, Random House – 2004, page 143
[30] Mark Essig, Edison and the Electric Chair: A Story of Light and Death, Bloomsbury Publishing USA – 2009, pages 139–140
[31] Mark Essig, Edison and the Electric Chair: A Story of Light and Death, Bloomsbury Publishing USA – 2009, page 268
[32] Robert L. Bradley Jr., Edison to Enron: Energy Markets and Political Strategies, John Wiley & Sons – 2011, pages 28–29
[33] Growing American Rubber by Mark Finlay
[34] Duke University Rare Book, Manuscript, and Special Collections Library: Edison fears the hidden perils of the x-rays. New York Worldb/, August 3, 1903, Durham, NC.
[35] Leonard–Cushing fight http://rs6.loc.gov/cgi-bin/query/r?ammem/papr:@filreq(@field(NUMBER+@band(edmp+4026))+@field(COLLID+edison)) Part of the Library of Congress/*Inventing Entertainment* educational website. Retrieved December 14, 2006.
[36] Siegmund Lubin (1851–1923) http://www.victorian-cinema.net/lubin.htm, Who's Who of Victorian Cinema. Retrieved August 20, 2007.
[37] "History of Edison Motion Pictures: Early Edison Motion Picture Production (1892–1895)" http://memory.loc.gov/ammem/edhtml/edmvhist1.html#EE, Memory.loc.gov, Library of Congress. Retrieved August 20, 2007.
[38] Reader's Digest, March 1930, pp. 1042–1044, "Living With a Genius", condensed from The American Magazine February 1930
[39] "Edison Wears Silk Nightshirt, Hates Talkies, Writes Wife", Capital Times, October 30, 1930
[40] Mann, Charles C. And Plummer, Mark L (1991)., The Aspirin Wars: Money, Medicine, and 100 Years of Rampant Competition, Alfred A. Knopf, NY, isbn 0-394-57894-5, p 38-40
[41] Conot, Robert (1979), A Streak of Luck: The Life & Legend of Thomas Alva Edison, Seaview Books, NY, p 413-4
[42] "Is Thomas Edison's last breath preserved in a test tube in the Henry Ford Museum?" http://www.straightdope.com/classics/a2_128a.html, The Straight Dope, September 11, 1987. Retrieved August 20, 2007.
[43] Neil Baldwin, Edison: Inventing the Century, University of Chicago Press – 2001, 408
[44] Baldwin 1995, p.60
[45] Baldwin 1995, p.67
[46] "The Life of Thomas Edison" http://memory.loc.gov/ammem/edhtml/edbio.html, *American Memory*, Library of Congress, Retrieved March 3, 2009.
[47] "Thomas Edison's First Wife May Have Died of a Morphine Overdose" http://news.rutgers.edu/medrel/research/rh-2011/thomas-edison2019s-f-20111115 , *Rutgers Today*. Retrieved November 18, 2011
[48] *The Freethinker https//books.google.com* (1970), G.W. Foote & Company, Volume 90, p. 147
[49] Cited in Innovate Like Edison: The Success System of America's Greatest Inventor https://books.google.com/books?id=DtjWFiDKsJ0C&pg=PA37&dq=%22Still+savages%22+edison&ei=KiHMSLJSiNzKBIiglYsJ&sig=ACfU3U2IXFOuvGUriygDwhEkgvqyaefwEg by Sarah Miller Caldicott, Michael J. Gelb, page 37.
[50] Edison, 1922
[51] NNDB online website http://www.nndb.com/honors/139/000048992/. The same decree awarded German physicist Hermann von Helmholtz with the designation of Grand Officer of the Legion of Honor, as well as Alexander Graham Bell. The decree preamble cited *"for services provided to the Congress and to the International Electrical Exhibition"*
[52] Menlo Park Museum, Tower-Restoration http://www.menloparkmuseum.org/tower-restoration . Retrieved September 28, 2010.
[53] Thomas Edison Depot http://www.phmuseum.org/drupal/about/depot . Retrieved September 28, 2010.
[54] Edison Memorial Fountain http://www.buildingsofdetroit.com/places/ef at Buildings of Detroit. Retrieved September 28, 2010.

[55] https://www.c-span.org/video/?63449-1/edison-inventing-century
[56] https://www.c-span.org/video/?178806-1/empires-light-edison-tesla-westinghouse
[57] https://web.archive.org/web/20070601215151/http://www.menloparkmuseum.com/
[58] http://www.nps.gov/edis/index.htm
[59] https://web.archive.org/web/20060424080435/http://www.hfmgv.org/exhibits/edison/
[60] http://www.edisonmuseum.org/
[61] https://web.archive.org/web/20060503223127/http://phmuseum.org/depot/depot.htm
[62] http://www.tomedison.org/
[63] http://www.edisonhouse.org/
[64] https://www.britannica.com/EBchecked/topic/179233
[65] http://www.bbc.co.uk/programmes/b00wdjr8
[66] https://www.youtube.com/watch?v=KgwY2SdRJ_4
[67] http://ariwatch.com/VS/TheDiaryOfThomasEdison.htm
[68] https://www.gutenberg.org/author/Edison,+Thomas+A.+(Thomas+Alva)
[69] https//archive.org
[70] https://www.archives.gov/exhibits/american_originals_iv/sections/thomas_edison_patent.html
[71] https://www.imdb.com/name/nm0249379/
[72] https://www.wired.com/science/discoveries/news/2008/01/dayintech_0104?
[73] http://www.nps.gov/nr/twhp/wwwlps/lessons/25edison/25edison.htm
[74] http://www.shapell.org/Collection/Historical-Figures/Edison-Thomas
[75] https://archive.org/details/gov.archives.arc.49442
[76] http://edison.rutgers.edu/
[77] http://www.edisonian.com/
[78] http://www.thomasedison.org
[79] https://www.findagrave.com/memorial/1630
[80] http://hfha.org/the-ford-story/the-illustrious-vagabonds
[81] https//books.google.com
[82] https://archive.org/details/filmcollectief-01-661
[83] https://www.youtube.com/watch?v=IfFIeUgt_7Q
[84] https://www.pbs.org/wgbh/americanexperience/films/light
[85] http://purl.org/pressemappe20/folder/pe/004481

Article Sources and Contributors

The sources listed for each article provide more detailed licensing information including the copyright status, the copyright owner, and the license conditions.

Thomas Edison *Source:* https://en.wikipedia.org/w/index.php?oldid=863118513 *License:* Creative Commons Attribution-Share Alike 3.0 *Contributors:* 7&6=thirteen, A Simple Name, A wild Rattata, Aboutmovies, Accurizer, Adem20, Adityaedits, Aidanbh, Akb332, AlanM1, Alansohn, Alexandritechrysoberyl, All Hallow's Wraith, Almodaa, Amscheip, Andy M. Wang, Another Believer, ArnoldReinhold, Arr4, Attic Salt, Audaciter, Autoenthusiast123, B14709, Ballymorey, Bananaword, Bender235, Bergeronp, Bigs7, Binksternet, Bomb319, Boydstra, Brentsalter, Britney901, CTF83!, Cannolis, Caroca2, Cartoon Boy, ChamithN, Chewings72, Chitt66, Chris the speller, Clayton Forrester, Clean Copy, ClueBot NG, Comfr, CommonsDelinker, Cruz charm, Curly Turkey, DBZFan30, Dagrenzer, Dale Arnett, Dawnseeker2000, Dcoetzee, Deisenbe, Dewritech, Dimadick, Dimsar01, Doctor Papa Jones, Don4of4, Doug Coldwell, Download, Dratman, Dstlascaux, Dthomsen8, ECayce187, Edhac-Edham, Elaqueate, Epalinurus, Epicgenius, Famartin, FeanorStar7, Figaro, FlightTime, Floquenbeam, Fountains of Bryn Mawr, Fredquint, FrenchieAlexandre, Frietjes, Gaius Cornelius, Galatz, GamerCat2016, Garfield7380, GennadyL, Gentlecollapse6, Giladsom, Glotof, Gothaparduskerialldrapolatkh, GreenC, Grubemeister, GünniX, HandsomeFella, Haxwell, Heididoerr061, Helgi-S, Heureka!, Higher Ground 1, History80, Hmains, Hoof Hearted, Hornpipe2, Ian3060, Icensnow42, Ikmarchini, J 1982, JackofOz, Jalco89, Jax 0677, Jmn100, Joan1066, Jobas, JoetheMoe25, John, Jon Kolbert, Jpgordon, KConWiki, Kablammo, Kailash29792, Kestenbaum, Kind Tennis Fan, Kkm010, Klichka, Kmcharw, Koplimek, Lebrsm, Linxit, Literalman, Lockesdonkey, LocusBeatus, Lovibond, MBlaze Lightning, Mabalu, Mackensen, Maczkopeti, Mandruss, Marcocapelle, Marek69, Martin "The Guru", Mary Mark Ockerbloom, Mawlidman, Maximajorian Viridio, Maynard-Clark, Mean as custard, Mndata, Mockingbird 1, Moviebuff1921, MrFrosty2, Mrhson, Muhammad Umair Mirza, Myconix, Nechemia Iron, Nick Number, Nick876436, Nodove, NottNott, Nwbeeson, Oceanflynn, Omio Asad, Omnipaedista, Opus88888, Ottawahitech, PMLawrence, Paine Ellsworth, PearlSt82, Peesaravanmuthudoubledeckerbus, Peter K Burian, Pjposullivan, Popcornduff, Prinsgezinde, Qed237, RJANKA, Racconish, Rachel123s, RagnaParadise, RainWizard29422, Randy Kryn, Rathfelder, Renamed user 8263928762779, Richard Arthur Norton (1958-), Rms125a@hotmail.com, Robertgombos, Rodw, Ryan Pikachu, SHCarter, SNUGGUMS, SVTCobra, SWM, SZN, Sailee5, Saintonge235, Scailhotrod, Ser Amantio di Nicolao, Shanaya1, SmartyBootz, Solntsa90, Sonicsuns, Spparky, Stardomax, Stevenmitchell, Steviethemen, Sudiani, Sundayclose, SwagMaster2030, Sylvain1972, T0mpr1c3, TAnthony, TDKR Chicago 101, TGCP, Tassedethe, TheQ Editor, Thumperward, TiMike, TonyTheTiger, Tpbradbury, Turkeybutt JC, Twocs, Usernameunique, Valetude, Vansh Bhardwaj, Vasyaivanov, Vektor00, Vincelord, Voxfax, Walk Like an Egyptian, Wayne Elgin, Wikiain, William Avery, Wnt, Wrath X, Wtshymanski, Yoho2001, Zero914, Zyxw 1

Image Sources, Licenses and Contributors

The sources listed for each image provide more detailed licensing information including the copyright status, the copyright owner, and the license conditions.

Image *Source:* https://en.wikipedia.org/w/index.php?title=File:Padlock-silver.svg *Contributors:* AzaToth, BotMultichill, BotMultichillT, Gurch, Jarekt, Kallerna, Multichill, Perhelion, Rd232, Riana, Sarang, Siebrand, Steinsplitter, 4 anonymous edits 1
Image *Source:* https://en.wikipedia.org/w/index.php?title=File:Thomas_Edison2.jpg *License:* Public Domain *Contributors:* Louis Bachrach, Bachrach Studios, restored by Michel Vuijlsteke 1
Image *Source:* https://en.wikipedia.org/w/index.php?title=File:Thomas_Alva_Edison_Signature.svg *License:* Public Domain *Contributors:* Bot-Multichill, BotMultichillT, Connormah, Davey2010, Eugenio Hansen, OFS, McSush, Myself488, 3 anonymous edits 1
Figure 1 *Source:* https://en.wikipedia.org/w/index.php?title=File:Young_Thomas_Edison.jpg *License:* Public Domain *Contributors:* Auntof6, Daderot, Infrogmation, JMCC1, Juliancolton, Junkyardsparkle, Maksim, Makthorpe, Martin H., Meno25, Succu, Túrelio, Vonvon, 13 anonymous edits 3
Figure 2 *Source:* https://en.wikipedia.org/w/index.php?title=File:Menlo_Park_Laboratory.JPG *License:* Creative Commons Attribution-Sharealike 2.5 *Contributors:* Andrew Balet 5
Figure 3 *Source:* https://en.wikipedia.org/w/index.php?title=File:Edison_and_phonograph_edit1.jpg *License:* Public Domain *Contributors:* Levin C. Handy (per http://hdl.loc.gov/loc.pnp/cwpbh.04326) 7
Image *Source:* https://en.wikipedia.org/w/index.php?title=File:Gnome-mime-sound-openclipart.svg *License:* *Contributors:* User:Eubulides 6
Figure 4 *Source:* https://en.wikipedia.org/w/index.php?title=File:Edison_bulb.jpg *License:* GNU Free Documentation License *Contributors:* Uploaded at enwp by User:Alkivar 9
Figure 5 *Source:* https://en.wikipedia.org/w/index.php?title=File:Light_bulb_Edison_2.jpg *License:* Public Domain *Contributors:* Thomas Edison (reprinted by the Norris Peters Co.) 10
Figure 6 *Source:* https://en.wikipedia.org/w/index.php?title=File:SS_Columbia_Undated_Photograph.png *License:* Public Domain *Contributors:* Blue Elf, MatthewAnderson707, OgreBot 2 11
Figure 7 *Source:* https://en.wikipedia.org/w/index.php?title=File:PyramidParthenon.jpg *License:* Public Domain *Contributors:* Hameryko, Infrogmation, J 1982, Kaldari, Xnatedawgx, 2 anonymous edits 12
Figure 8 *Source:* https://en.wikipedia.org/w/index.php?title=File:Edison_battery_exhibit._1915.jpg *License:* Public Domain *Contributors:* CourtlyHades296, Davey2010, OgreBot 2, Tillman 14
Figure 9 *Source:* https://en.wikipedia.org/w/index.php?title=File:Leonard_Cushing_Kinetograph_1894.ogv *License:* Public Domain *Contributors:* William Heise 16
Figure 10 *Source:* https://en.wikipedia.org/w/index.php?title=File:A_day_with_Thomas_A._Edison.webm *License:* Public Domain *Contributors:* Racconish 18
Figure 11 *Source:* https://en.wikipedia.org/w/index.php?title=File:Edison_Storage_Battery_Company_1903.JPG *Contributors:* Unbekannte Autoren und Grafiker; Scan vom EDHAC e.V. 19
Figure 12 *Source:* https://en.wikipedia.org/w/index.php?title=File:EFWE_2008.04.01_.jpg *Contributors:* User:Amscheip 20
Figure 13 *Source:* https://en.wikipedia.org/w/index.php?title=File:Ford_Edison_Firestone1.jpg *License:* Public Domain *Contributors:* Daderot, Lotje, Mutter Erde, Nczempin, Robfergusonjr 22
Figure 14 *Source:* https://en.wikipedia.org/w/index.php?title=File:Mina_Edison_1906.jpg *License:* Public Domain *Contributors:* Pach Bros. .. 24
Figure 15 *Source:* https://en.wikipedia.org/w/index.php?title=File:Abraham_Archibald_Anderson_-_Thomas_Alva_Edison_-_Google_Art_Project.jpg *Contributors:* Boo-Boo Baroo, BoringHistoryGuy, Coyau, Ecummenic, HCShannon, JMCC1, Laura1822, Mabrndt, Mattes, Multichill, OgreBot 2 27
Figure 16 *Source:* https://en.wikipedia.org/w/index.php?title=File:Thomas_Edison_3c_1947_issue_U.S._stamp.jpg *License:* Public Domain *Contributors:* EurekaLott, JMCC1, MrFrosty2, Robert Weemeyer 28
Figure 17 *Source:* https://en.wikipedia.org/w/index.php?title=File:Thomas_Edison_1.jpg *License:* Creative Commons Attribution-Sharealike 3.0 *Contributors:* User:Mabrgordon 29
Figure 18 *Source:* https://en.wikipedia.org/w/index.php?title=File:Эдисон_Томас_Альва_фото_ЖЗЛ.JPG *License:* Public Domain *Contributors:* Daderot, Grunpfnul, Quibik, Vizu 31
Image *Source:* https://en.wikipedia.org/w/index.php?title=File:Nuvola_apps_kaboodle.svg *License:* GNU Lesser General Public License *Contributors:* David Vignoni / ICON KING 33
Image *Source:* https://en.wikipedia.org/w/index.php?title=File:Commons-logo.svg *License:* logo *Contributors:* Anomie, Callanecc, CambridgeBay-Weather, Jo-Jo Eumerus, RHaworth 35
Image *Source:* https://en.wikipedia.org/w/index.php?title=File:Wikiquote-logo.svg *License:* Public Domain *Contributors:* Rei-artur 35
Image *Source:* https://en.wikipedia.org/w/index.php?title=File:Wikisource-logo.svg *License:* Creative Commons Attribution-Sharealike 3.0 *Contributors:* ChrisiPK, Guillom, INeverCry, Jarekt, JuTa, Leyo, Lokal Profil, MichaelMaggs, NielsF, Rei-artur, Rocket000, Romaine, Steinsplitter 35

License

Creative Commons Attribution-Share Alike 3.0
//creativecommons.org/licenses/by-sa/3.0/

Index

Abraham Archibald Anderson, 27
Acid-base extraction, 19
Acoustical Society of America, 17
Akron, Ohio, 23
Alessandro Volta, 8
Alexander Graham Bell, 7, 8, 38
Alices Adventures in Wonderland (1910 film), 17
Alternating current, 12
Alva, Florida, 29
American Institute of Electrical Engineers, 27, 31
American Magazine, 25
American Mutoscope and Biograph, 17
Americans, 1
American Society of Mechanical Engineers, 31
Ammonium picrate, 20, 21
Aniline dyes, 20
Applications, 7
Arc lamp, 12
Arthur E. Kennelly, 33
Aspirin, 21
Associated Press, 4
Asteroid, 29
Atheism, 25
Austria-Hungary, 17
Automotive Hall of Fame, 30

Bakelite, 20, 21
Bamboo, 9
Bayer, 21
BBC, 35
B. C. Forbes, 25
Beaumont, Texas, 30
Bell Telephone Company, 8
Benzene, 20
Bessemer, AL, 20
Botany, 2
Brain tumor, 23
Brno, 11
Businessman, 1

California, 29
Carbon, 9

Carbonization, 9
Carbon microphone, 7, 8
Charles Batchelor, 32
Charles Edison, 1, 23
Charles Sumner Tainter, 7
Chautauqua Institution, 23
Chemische Fabrik von Heyden, 21
Chenango County, New York, 2
Chichester Bell, 7
Civitan International, 21
Clara Bow, 17
Clarence Madison Dally, 15
Coal, 20
Coke oven, 20
Commonwealth Edison, 30
Congressional Gold Medal, 27
Consolidated Edison, 30
Continental Divide, 9
C-SPAN, 33

David Edward Hughes, 8
Dearborn, Michigan, 30
Death mask, 23
Deism, 25
Delaware, Lackawanna and Western Railroad, 21
Design patent, 6
Detroit Edison, 30
Diabetes, 2
Direct current, 12
Dover, New Jersey, 21
DTE Energy, 30

Edison Award, 31
Edison Bridge (Florida), 29
Edison Bridge (New Jersey), 29
Edison Bridge (Ohio), 29
Edison Building (Falconbridge), 18
Edison Electric Institute, 30
Edison Electric Light Company, 9
Edison High School (disambiguation), 28
Edison Illuminating Company, 12, 32
Edison International, 30
Edison Machine Works, 32, 33

Edison Manufacturing Company, 33
Edison Medal, 31
Edison Museum, 30
Edison National Historic Site, 30
Edison, New Jersey, 4, 28
Edison Ore-Milling Company, 5, 18, 30
Edison Portland Cement Company, 30
Edisons Black Maria, 2, 30
Edison S.p.A., 30
Edison State College, 28
Edison Studios, 17
Ediswan, 11
Edward Goodrich Acheson, 32
Edward Hibberd Johnson, 33
Edward H. Johnson, 5
Edward Longstreth Medal, 26
Edwin Stanton Porter, 33
Electrical engineering, 31
Electrical resistance and conductance, 8
Electric chair, 14
Electric current, 8
Electricity distribution, 12
Electric power generation, 2
Electrocuting an Elephant, 17
Electrodeless lamp, 10
Elihu Thomson, 31
Elizabeth, New Jersey, 4
Emile Berliner, 8
Encyclopædia Britannica, 35
Entrepreneur Walk of Fame, 28
Exelon, 30

Fairs, 17
Falconbridge, Greater Sudbury, Ontario, 18
Falconbridge Ltd., 18
File:Thomas Edison Mary had lamb.ogg, 6
Film studio, 2
Find a Grave, 36
First Energy, 30
Florida SouthWestern State College, 28
Fluoroscopy, 15
Food faddism, 22
Fort Myers, Florida, 2, 14
Francis Jehl, 11, 33
Francis Robbins Upton, 5, 33
Frankenstein (1910 film), 17
Frank J. Sprague, 5, 33
Franklin Leonard Pope, 4
Franklin Medal, 27
Fred Otts Sneeze, 17
Freethought, 25
French Third Republic, 26
Ft. Myers, 22

Gaslighting, 20
General Electric, 4, 14, 30

Genius, 7
George F. Morrison, 33
George Westinghouse, 10, 13
German dye trust, 21
German National Library of Economics, 36
Gladstone, New Jersey, 21
Gleaves class destroyer, 32
Google, 32
Google Doodle, 32
Governor of New Jersey, 23
Grand Circus Park Historic District, 30
Grand Trunk Railway, 3
Greater Sudbury, 18
Great Floridian, 28
Great Phenol, 21
Gutenberg:820, 36

Hammer Historical Collection of Incandescent
    Electric Lamps, 5
Harold P. Brown, 13
Harvey Firestone, 2, 22
Heinrich Göbel, 8
Helena Blavatsky, 25
Help:Media, 6
Henry Ford, 2, 19, 21, 22, 26, 32
Henry Ford Museum, 5
Henry Villard, 10
Henry Woodward (inventor), 8
Hermann von Helmholtz, 38
High explosive, 20
Hoboken, New Jersey, 21
Holborn Viaduct, 12
Hotel Edison, 29
Hotel Edison (Sunbury, Pennsylvania), 29
Humphry Davy, 8

IMDb, 35
Incandescent light bulb, 2, 5, 29
Industrial society, 2
In Our Time (radio series), 35
Institute of Electrical and Electronics Engi-
    neers, 31
Interest, 26
International Standard Book Number, 33–35
Internet Archive, 35, 36
Inventor, 1, 2
Inventors Day, 27
Irving T. Bush, 16

James Bowman Lindsay, 8
Johann Philipp Reis, 8
John Eyre Sloane, 23
John Fritz Medal, 27
John I. Beggs, 32
John Kruesi, 33
John Scott Medal, 26

46

Johnstown, PA, 20
John W. Lieb, 33
Joseph Swan, 8
Joules first law, 6
J. P. Morgan, 9
J.P. Morgan, 14
Jules Barthélemy-Saint-Hilaire, 26
Jules Grévy, 26
Justus B. Entz, 32

Kinetoscope, 16
Kunihiko Iwadare, 33

Lake Thomas A Edison, 29
Lead–acid battery, 4
Légion dhonneur, 26
Legion of Honour, 26
Leon Gaumont, 17
Leon Trotsky, 36
Lewis Howard Latimer, 33
Lewis Latimer, 10
Lewis Miller (philanthropist), 1, 23
Library of Congress, 38
Life (magazine), 28
Light bulb, 28
List of Edison patents, 2
List of People on the Cover of Time Magazine: 1920s, 36
List of prolific inventors, 2
Llewellyn Park, 14, 23
Louis Adolphe Cochery, 26
Louisiana Purchase Exposition, 27
Louisville, Kentucky, 4
Loyalist (American Revolution), 2
Luna Park, Coney Island (1903), 17

Madeleine Edison, 1
Mahen Theatre, 11
Manhattan, 12
Manufactured gas, 20
Marshalltown, Nova Scotia, 2
Mary Pickford, 17
Mass communication, 2
Mass production, 2
Mathew Brady, 7
Mathew Evans, 8
Matteucci Medal, 26
Matthew Josephson, 37
Menlo Park, New Jersey, 2, 4
Methodist, 23
Microphone, 7
Middlesex County, New Jersey, 4
Midwest, 2
Milan, Ohio, 1, 2, 22
Miller Reese Hutchison, 32
Minister of Foreign Affairs (France), 26

Minister of Posts, Telegraphs, and Telephones (France), 26
Montclair, New Jersey, 21
Morphine overdose, 23
Moses G. Farmer, 8
Motion Picture Patents Company, 17
Motion pictures, 2
Mount Clemens, Michigan, 3
Movie camera, 2

National Academy of Sciences, 27
National Park Service, 30
National Portrait Gallery (United States), 27
National Statuary Hall Collection, 30
Naval Consulting Board, 15
Navy Distinguished Service Medal, 27
Neil Baldwin (writer), 37
Newark, New Jersey, 6
New Jersey Hall of Fame, 28
New Jersey Transit, 22
News agency, 4
New York City, 10, 29
New York Times Magazine, 25
Nikola Tesla, 32, 33
Non-profit foundation, 36
Nonviolence, 25

Ohms Law, 6
Oregon Railroad and Navigation Company, 10, 11
Overhead lines, 12

Parliament, 20
Pearl Street (Manhattan), 12
Pearl Street Station, 12
Pelé, 29
Phenol, 20
Phenolic resins, 20
Philadelphia City Council, 26
Philip Diehl (inventor), 10
Phonograph, 2, 6, 20
Photographic paper, 17
Picric acid, 20
Piqua, Ohio, 28
Piscataway, NJ, 21
Plastic, 21
Platinocyanide, 15
Platinum, 9
Popular culture, 32
Popular Mechanics, 36
Port Huron, Michigan, 2, 3, 30
Port Huron Museum, 30
P-phenylenediamine, 21
President of France, 26
Prior art, 6
Project Gutenberg, 35, 36

Propaganda, 13
Public company, 4
Public utility, 12
Pyrax, 21

Quadruplex telegraph, 4

Radiographs, 15
Rebellions of 1837, 2
Reginald Fessenden, 32
Rensselaer, NY, 21
Research laboratory, 2
Richard Swann Lull, 36
Roasted, 8
Roselle, New Jersey, 12
Royal Swedish Academy of Sciences, 26

Salicylic acid, 21
Samuel Insull, 33
Sarnia, 2
Scarlet fever, 3
Scheelite, 15
School of Natural Philosophy, 2
Self-educated, 1
Seminole Lodge (Thomas Edison), 15
Shellac, 21
Silver Lake, NJ, 20
Sir Joshua Reynolds, 6
Smear campaign, 14
Smiths Creek, Michigan, 3
Snake oil, 24
Solidago leavenworthii, 15
Sound quality, 7
Sound recording, 2
Southern California Edison, 30
South Orange, NJ, 22
Southwestern Ontario, 2
Spencer Trask, 9
SS Columbia (1880), 10, 11
Station master, 3
St. Clair River, 30
Stephen J. Herben, 23
Sulfuric acid, 4
Sunbury, Pennsylvania, 29

Talkies, 17
Technical Grammy Award, 28
Telegraph operator, 2
Tennessee Centennial Exposition, 12
The Age of Reason, 25
The Birth of a Nation, 17
The Cooper Union for the Advancement of Science and Art, 2
The Franklin Institute, 26, 27
The Greatest American, 28
The Great Train Robbery (1903 film), 17

The Henry Ford, 23, 30
The Kiss (1896 film), 17
Theodore Miller Edison, 1, 23
The Order and other countries, 26
Theosophical Society, 25
Thermoset, 21
The Straight Dope, 38
Thomas A. Edison Middle School, 29
Thomas Alva Edison Memorial Tower and Museum, 30
Thomas Armat, 16
Thomas Commerford Martin, 33
Thomas Edison, **1**, 35
Thomas Edison (Cottrill), 30
Thomas Edison Depot Museum, 30
Thomas Edison Jr.s activities, 1
Thomas Edison National Historical Park, 1, 14
Thomas Edison State University, 28
Thomas Paine, 25
Thomson-Houston Electric Company, 13, 30
Ticker tape, 15
Topsy (elephant), 17
Transformer, 13
Trenton, New Jersey, 28

United Kingdom, 20
United States, 29
United States Capitol, 30
United States Congress, 27
United States Navy, 5, 27, 32
United States Patent and Trademark Office, 11
Upper Canada, 2
U.S. copyright office, 17
USS Edison (DD-439), 32
USS Thomas A. Edison (SSBN-610), 32

Vanderbilt family, 9
Vegan, 25
Vegetarian, 25
Vienna, Ontario, 2
Vitascope, 16

War of 1812, 2
War of Currents, 14
Washington Post, 7
Western Union, 4, 8
Westinghouse Electric (1886), 13
West Orange, New Jersey, 1, 2, 14, 23
Wikipedia:Citation needed, 22, 30, 32
Wikisource, 35
Wikisource:Author:Thomas Edison, 35
Wilhelm Röntgen, 15
William Allen (governor), 30
William E. Sawyer, 8, 11
William Joseph Hammer, 5, 32
William Kennedy Dickson, 32

William Symes Andrews, 32
Wired (magazine), 35
Worlds fair, 27
World War I, 15, 20
Wyoming, 9
W. K. L. Dickson, 16

X-rays, 15
Xylene, 21

YouTube, 36

www.ingramcontent.com/pod-product-compliance
Lightning Source LLC
Chambersburg PA
CBHW031947070426
42453CB00007BA/504